G000244040

A turnover shawl of the 1860s, using two borders from Clabburn & Crisp shawls. A turnover was fashionable in the 1830s and 1840s but this method of using up spare borders has worked very well. (Private collection)

SHAWLS

PAMELA CLABBURN

A SHIRE BOOK

Published in 2002 by Shire Publications Ltd,
Cromwell House, Church Street, Princes Risborough,
Buckinghamshire HP27 9AA, UK.
(Website: www.shirebooks.co.uk)

British Library Cataloguing in Publication Data:
Clabburn, Pamela
Shawls. – 2nd ed. – (A Shire book)
1. Shawls - Great Britain – History
2. Shawl industry – Great Britain – History
I. Title 391.2
ISBN 0 7478 0524 5

Cover: *A beautiful turnover shawl, c.1835, with the design in the Richard Shaw pattern book (see page 37). The trailing green stalk is a recurring theme in various guises in Shaw's work. (Carrow House Textile Collection. Norfolk Museums 51.951.3)*

ACKNOWLEDGEMENTS
Many friends and colleagues have helped with this book. Since the first edition appeared in 1981 much more has been discovered about the shawl industry in Britain generally and in Norwich in particular. Many shawls in private hands have come to light and their owners have been most generous in recounting their history as far as is known and allowing them to be photographed. Other friends have helped with their specialised knowledge of weaving and printing, and I can only hope that they are happy with this book. My special thanks go to Helen Hoyte, who took many of the photographs and wrote the chapter on printed shawls; Judy Wentworth, whose criticism was unsparing and helpful; Eileen Collisson, whose knowledge of the whereabouts of shawls in Carrow House was invaluable; and most of all to all the workers at Carrow House, both professional and lay, who put up with my demands for space in which to work and helped in every way possible.

Printed in Malta by Gutenberg Press Limited, Gudja Road,
Tarxien PLA 19, Malta.

CONTENTS

'The Little Norwich Shawl Worker', engraved by Thomas Overton in 1826 after the painting by Joseph Clover, 1815.

INTRODUCTION

It is not often realised that until 1662 the word *shawl* had never been written in Britain and at that date it referred only to the scarves and girdles worn by Persian and Indian men. Not until 1767 was it used to refer to an article of dress worn by a European.

Before the advent of the shawl women wore some kind of cloak or cape, with or without a hood, for warmth and protection from the weather. Only in the second half of the seventeenth century, when

ships trading with the East brought back oblongs of fine woollen fabric woven with unfamiliar colourful designs, was there any thought of change. It appears that in Europe this item, then known as a *schal*, *scial* or *chal*, was not immediately used for clothing but was probably kept to be admired or used as a light rug. It was not until the last quarter of the eighteenth century that shawls began to be appropriated by all women, from the wealthiest aristocrat to the humblest kitchenmaid, as beautiful, exotic and practical adjuncts to feminine dress.

This book examines shawls in the three largest centres of manufacture in Britain, namely Norwich, Edinburgh and Paisley, but they were also made in larger quantities in France, Russia and central Europe as well as in India.

Left: A *Jacquard loom in the Bridewell Museum, Norwich, used for shawl-weaving in the nineteenth century.*

Two wooden blocks for printing shawls. (Bridewell Museum, Norwich)

A superb shawl, probably a 'one off', named 'the Bishop's wife's shawl' at Carrow House. The crosses are more ecclesiastical than merely decorative, and any help in tracing its provenance would be welcomed.

Advertising card of P. J. Knights, Shawl Manufacturer to Her Majesty. In 1792–3 the firm was still experimenting with shawl bed furniture, dresses, scarves, shawls, fancy waistcoats, riding cravats, etc. (Carrow House Textile Collection. Norfolk Museums)

The front and back of a woven Norwich shawl, 1840s. (Carrow House Textile Collection. Norfolk Museums 40.942.2)

5

INDIAN SHAWLS

It is convenient to use the term *Indian shawl* as British manufacturers generally referred to their shawls as Indian, labelling some of their designs and advertising them as 'in imitation of the Indian', but only some of the shawls they were imitating were made in the north of India while a large number were made in Kashmir. The Kashmiri shawls were woven from some of the softest and finest wool in the world, from the fleece of the mountain goat (*Capra hircus*) which lives high in the Himalayas. The goat sheds its wool fleece, known as *pashmina*, at the beginning of summer; this was collected and taken to the weavers in Kashmir, who spun and wove it into the finest (and most expensive) shawls. The next best wool came from the flocks of domesticated goats herded by nomadic tribes and this was used by the weavers in northern India.

The Indian weavers wove their shawls very slowly indeed, sometimes taking as long as eighteen months on one shawl. The method they used was the same as for European tapestry weaving, where the pattern is put in with a separate shuttle for each colour, which goes only as far as the pattern requires and then turns back – it does not go across the whole width of the warp. In the Indian weave, however, the ground is a twill instead of a plain weave. Indian shawls were generally woven in pairs, the two shawls being worn back to back. Even with the weavers' poor rate of pay, the slow method made the shawls very expensive by the time they reached Europe.

One of the most characteristic designs of these shawls was the *buta* (flower), which was first a small plant and then developed into an elegant, stylised vase or tied bunch of flowers. It became gradually formalised into a tight bunch within a shape which resembled a pine cone with a bent tip, and it was this which became one of the most widely copied and adapted patterns in Europe and which eventually, when Paisley was producing its greatest number of shawls, became known as the Paisley pattern.

Except for the ground colour, petunia instead of red, this shawl might well be Indian but it is probably from Norwich, 1825–30. (Carrow House Textile Collection. Norfolk Museums 173.979)

SHAWLS IN BRITAIN IN THE EIGHTEENTH CENTURY

Indian shawls were reaching Britain in small numbers through the early years of the eighteenth century, either being imported by the East India Company or being brought home by returning Anglo-Indians as presents. In retrospect it is surprising that none of the diarists or letter-writers of that time mentions them and it seems probable that the shawls were not thought of as articles of dress but as beautiful textiles. There are no portraits from this period of ladies wearing them; indeed, their soft and supple qualities of drapery would not have gone well with the stiff silks that were the hallmark of fashionable dressing until the 1780s. During the last quarter of the eighteenth century, with the emergence of cotton as a fashionable fabric, the female silhouette changed to a softer and narrower line, which was much more suited to the wearing of a shawl.

Shawl-making in Britain began between 1775 and 1785 in two main centres, Edinburgh and Norwich, but the early history is fragmentary. In Edinburgh it can mainly be gleaned from a study of the minutes of the Scottish Board of Trustees for Agriculture and

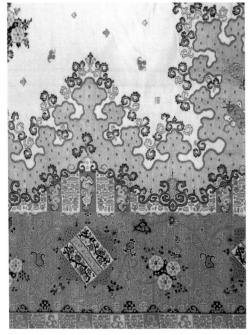

A fascinating shawl of unknown origin. The heavy line round the main design looks as though it has been embroidered, and the tiny motifs on the ground and angular squares in the border should be possible to interpret, but so far without success. (Private collection)

Fisheries (also concerned with textiles) and the *First Statistical Account of Scotland*, while in Norwich there are references in various letters and accounts, and the many advertisements in the *Norwich Mercury* and *Norfolk Chronicle* tell a great deal, even allowing for the self-aggrandisement of the retailers and manufacturers. It becomes clear that the infant trade did well, with both centres making great efforts to improve the quality of the manufacture and develop a worthwhile product.

Edinburgh was famous for its woven linen damasks and it appears that one such manufacturer, William Mortimer, wove the first shawls there. By 1791 minutes of the Board of Trustees refer to a petition from one George Richmond, 'Manufacturer of Shawls at Sciennes', who states that he has thirteen looms working but needs extra supplies of yarn and machinery for 'weaving upon the Shawls figures like the Indian', which, at this date, probably meant the small compact flower patterns – called *spades* in Scotland. From 1795 the Board of Trustees was giving premiums or prizes for shawls 'made in imitation of the Indian'. Apparently these shawls had their designs printed or brocaded.

In Norwich in 1791 one retailer was selling 'Norwich and other shawls equal in beauty and wear to those imported from the East Indies', and in the next year, 1792, a firm of hatters and hosiers advertises that 'being connected in the manufacture of Norwich shawls [it has] always ready for the inspection of the public a large and general assortment of every Article in that branch, of the richest patterns and very best fabric, viz: Shawl Cravats, Sashes, Waistcoat Shapes, 6/4ths square shawls, 3/4th and 4/4 scarfs and gown-pieces in great variety'. Measurement at this date was in quarter yards (9 inches), so 6/4th square equalled 54 inches or 1.36 metres square.

This and similar advertisements show that in Norwich, at least, manufacturers were thinking of shawls in terms of fabric rather than as articles of dress and were ready to use this fabric for other things, including upholstery and furnishings. This is borne out by the

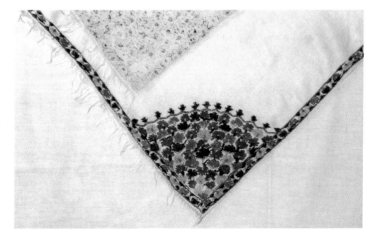

The back and front of an early Norwich shawl with the design darned in by hand, c.1800. (Carrow House Textile Collection. Norfolk Museums 2000.136)

The centrepiece of the Norwich shawl counterpane with the Royal Arms embroidered with running stitch, 1792. (Carrow House Textile Collection. Norfolk Museums)

advertisements of P.J. Knights, a manufacturer who was adept at self-promotion. After winning a silver medal from the Royal Society of Arts in 1792 for a shawl counterpane woven '4 yards square without seams', he went on to weave shawl fabric for the Duke of Norfolk. The *Norfolk Chronicle* reports that the Duke visited an 'Exhibition of Mr Knights' Shawl Manufactory' and 'assured Mr Knights he should furnish three new rooms in Arundel Castle with shawl manufacture and expressed it as his particular wish that every part of the furniture should be executed in Norfolk, desiring Mr Knights to find every part of it complete viz: cabinet works, carving, gilding, upholstery, etc.'. After presenting one of his shawl counterpanes to Queen Charlotte, the wife of George III, Knights was appointed 'Shawl-man to Her Majesty', and in December 1792 it was reported that 'On Saturday last Her Majesty and all the Princesses appeared in Norwich Shawl Dresses of Mr Knights' Manufactury'.

Only two of Knights's shawl counterpanes are known, though there must have been others. One is the prototype of that made for Queen Charlotte, with the royal coat of arms darned in as a centrepiece, now in the Textile and Costume Study Centre, Carrow House, Norwich. The other, with the arms of the second Earl of Buckingham and his second wife, Caroline Connolly, was cut up and used as the headboard and valance in the Chinese bedroom at Blickling Hall, Norfolk. Both counterpanes are very finely woven with a silk warp and a fine wool weft.

The designs of these two counterpanes have little resemblance to Indian designs, consisting as they do of the arms of the families for whom they were intended, but the border of the Blickling counterpane does have a Persian-looking bunch of flowers alternating with shields of various collateral families. From these two examples and from various other references it is clear that, unlike the printed or brocaded Edinburgh shawls, the design on all early Norwich shawls was darned in, the darning stitches being so close that at a short distance the design appeared to be woven. Even as late as 1827 an article on tambouring in Scotland in the *Encyclopaedia Edinensis* states that darning 'has been frequently much in demand, probably from its striking resemblance of Indian manufacture. The workmanship on the borders and corners of the fine worsted shawls manufactured at Norwich is of this kind, and is perhaps the happiest imitation of Indian workmanship that we have in this country.'

By 1795 the wrap had become an article of fashion and Norwich manufacturers were starting to concentrate entirely on shawls rather than diversifying into shawl fabrics. In 1796 John Bidwell could write to his partner: 'Our shawl trade is wonderfully brisk. Have now 18 looms at work and could employ without any exaggeration 3 or 4 times as many.' And, as a London wholesaler wrote to the same man: 'Mr Bidwell [has] been so full of the Shawl trade that he gave me orders in London not to take any more orders as he can sell 10 times more than he can make ...'. The shawl trade was beginning to boom.

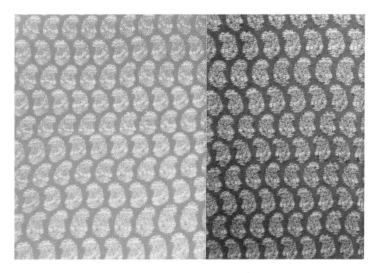

Two early shawls, c.1810, identical in design but with markedly different grounds. They are said to have been manufactured by E. & F. Hinde, a firm that started in Norwich in 1810, and are of silk warps and wool weft, very harsh to the touch but accurately woven. (Carrow House Textile Collection. Norfolk Museums 617.972.1 and 293.974.2)

SHAWLS IN BRITAIN IN
THE NINETEENTH CENTURY

By 1800 women's dresses were generally made of muslin and fine cotton and a shawl became a useful adjunct both for warmth and for the splash of colour it gave to the mainly white clothing. It also became a fashionable, as distinct from a utilitarian, article after Napoleon and his army returned from the Egyptian campaign of 1798 with Indian shawls as presents for their womenfolk. Even though Britain was at war with France, the British still considered the French as leaders in the world of fashion and when, during the short-lived peace in 1802, they flocked to Paris they saw many of these superb articles. The paintings of Ingres in particular show just how richly coloured and beautiful the shawls could be.

In the early years of the nineteenth century shawl-weaving was still very tentative, with various types and designs being tried out according to the fashion in dress and the capability of the various looms. Generally, they were either long with a deep border at each end and a narrow border along the sides, or square with often a plain silk centre and a narrow border round the edge. The long shawl was sometimes worn round the shoulders but was often draped across

It is debatable whether this early square turnover shawl, c.1810, is from Edinburgh or Norwich. The single bunch of flowers in each corner has been applied with black tambouring. (Private collection)

Above: A woven silk shawl, probably from Edinburgh, c.1810. (Private collection)

Right: A striking long shawl with silk ground of unknown provenance. The design of 'seahorses' and 'flying' motifs is very unusual but very effective. Probably Scottish, c.1815–20. (Private collection)

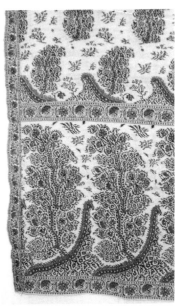

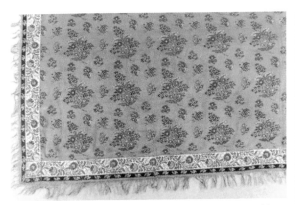

Above: Elizabeth Bolingbroke bought this shawl in Norwich to wear at her wedding in 1815. Unfortunately she did not mention the manufacturer in her letter. Silk twill ground with wool fillover. (Carrow House Textile Collection. Norfolk Museums)

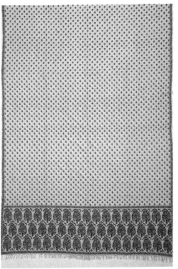

the back and over the elbows, with the decorative ends hanging down on either side of the dress. The border of the square shawls was often sewn on so that two adjoining sides faced one way and the other two were reversed. This meant that when a shawl was folded diagonally and worn round the shoulders both borders would appear on the right side and could be arranged one above the other, showing twice as much pattern. These were known as *turnover* shawls.

Above: A long shawl of unknown provenance. Its date is known because 'M. R. Dawson 1827' is embroidered on one side. (Carrow House Textile Collection. Norfolk Museums 185.965)

Right: *Long shawl, Edinburgh, 1830. Woven by the firm of Gibb & Macdonald of Edinburgh. (Private collection)*

Below: *A delightful woven long shawl with a pointed Christmas-tree design found in several other shawls, probably 1840. Origin unknown. (Private collection)*

Below: *A square shawl, 1840s, with silk warp and wool weft. Possibly made by Willett & Nephew, Norwich. (Private collection)*

13

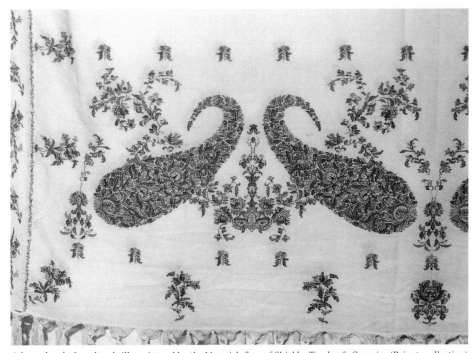

A long shawl of wool and silk registered by the Norwich firm of Shickle, Towler & Campin. (Private collection)

By the 1820s the fashion for shawls was becoming such that no woman with any pretension to elegance would be without several to match her different *toilettes*, and in spite of various peaks and recessions, particularly the recession of 1826, the manufacturers were keeping pace with the demand. In the late eighteenth and early nineteenth centuries it is clear that in Edinburgh, Norwich and, later, Paisley the manufacture of shawls had been ancillary to the ordinary weaving industries of mainly linen damasks in Edinburgh, worsteds and half-silks in Norwich, and muslins and gauzes in Paisley. It was only from about 1820 that Paisley became the biggest centre of shawl production; from the early 1840s it turned almost exclusively to shawl manufacture. In

A well-designed long shawl, Paisley, 1840–50. (Paisley Museum and Art Galleries)

A Norwich turnover shawl embroidered by hand, c.1800. (Carrow House Textile Collection. Norfolk Museums 1998.536)

Left: *A plain turnover shawl with a narrow border and a long untidy fringe, probably from Norwich, 1810–20. (Private collection)*

Below: *An Edinburgh turnover shawl with applied corner pines, 1840. (Private collection)*

Norwich some manufacturers produced only shawls, while others wove both shawls and textiles such as bombazine, camlet, barège and challis. In 1801 there were sixteen manufacturers weaving shawls, some exclusively and some together with other products. The increased trade was very welcome as orders from the East India Company for camlets declined, and more and more Norwich manufacturers turned to shawls, with varying fortunes. The trade in Edinburgh by the 1840s had gradually died out and production in the north became confined to Paisley.

Between 1820 and 1850 skirts increased in width, culminating in the very large crinolines of the 1850s and 1860s, and the wearing of a shawl became more of

Left: *A long brilliant pink scarf, from Paisley or Norwich, 1815–20; silk warp ground with wool and cotton fillover. (Private collection)*

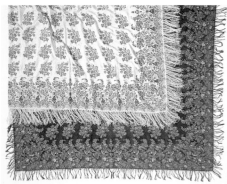

Right: *Two shawls of identical design but with different ground colour, 1815–20. (Carrow House Textile Collection. Norfolk Museums 617.972.1 and 293.974.2)*

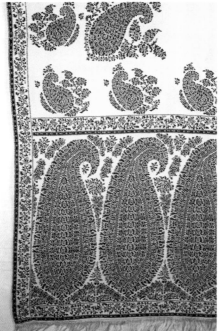

Below: *A stole, silk and wool, probably Scottish, 1820s. (Private collection)*

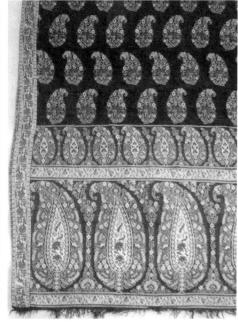

Above: *This woven long shawl of the 1820s resembles a 'pale-end' or kirking shawl but was probably made in Norwich. (Carrow House Textile Collection. Norfolk Museums 458.961)*

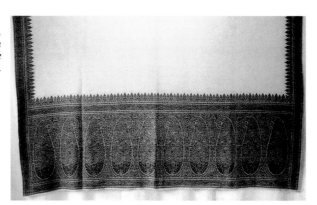

A kirking shawl, from Edinburgh, c.1840s. A heavy border with ten large voided pines and only three colours: two blues and a little red. (Private collection)

a necessity owing to the difficulty of wearing any shape of coat over the wide sleeves and cumbersome skirts. This was the heyday of the shawl and manufacturers responded. They could produce more complex patterns on the Jacquard looms and tried many different styles. The order book of one firm in Norwich, E. & F. Hinde, lists twenty-six styles for 1847–8, most of which can only be guessed today, and the book also shows that in that year they sold 32,000 shawls, of which over four thousand went to one buyer. Designs were printed as well as woven, on light leno and gauze fabrics for summer and on wool for winter. The summer shawls were high fashion but those of printed wool were produced in quantity for the cheaper end of the market.

Left: A shawl with decorative strips with small motifs either side; the double edges and the flower petals are unusual. Probably made by Willett & Nephew of Norwich, 1830s. (Private collection)

Right: A shawl of printed wool, with the fringe added with three rows of running stitch, c.1830. Some of the motifs have been coloured using the 'rainbow' technique, a method which allowed two colours to merge one into the other at the edges, using only one block. Origin unknown. (Private collection)

By 1847 shawls had ceased to be woven in Edinburgh, but in the period 1840–70 Paisley, Norwich and other centres in Europe, especially France and Austria, were producing shawls of every type and kind, many of them still 'in imitation of the Indian'. By the end of the 1860s, however, the fashion was beginning to change. It is interesting to note that in the *Englishwoman's Domestic Magazine* for 1869 there are two apparently conflicting observations on shawls. One writer had been to see the many new Indian shawls at Farmers & Rogers Shawl Emporium in Regent Street in London and declared: 'the outdoor article *par excellence* for our changeable climate is the

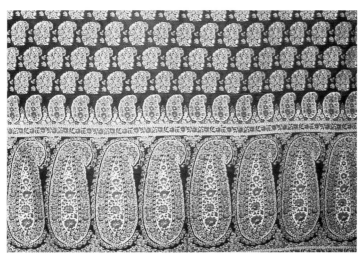

A Paisley shawl with 'spade' pattern, with all the pines facing the same way, 1830–40. (Paisley Museum and Art Galleries)

A light and charming long shawl of wool and silk, resembling other shawls by Towler & Campin of Norwich, 1840s. (Private collection)

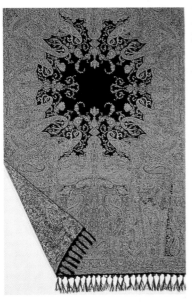

Left: *A long shawl with a dense pattern designed by W. S. Morrison of Norwich in 1848; the firm for which he worked is not known. (Carrow House Textile Collection. Norfolk Museums 3.968.1)*

Above: *A 'compartment' centre plaid, c.1855. (Paisley Museum and Art Galleries 149/1964)*

Above: *An all-over-pattern shawl, c.1860. (Paisley Museum and Art Galleries 165/1964)*

Right: *Detail of an all-over plaid, c.1865. (Paisley Museum and Art Galleries PS32)*

19

One of the few shawls known from the firm of John Sultzer of Norwich, c.1880. A good block-printed design has been spoilt by a ragged fringe of black knitting wool. (Carrow House Textile Collection. Norfolk Museums 10.969)

shawl … Graceful and *dégagé*, the shawl will retain its place in our toilettes when the ephemeral costumes and fancy dresses are forgotten or laughed at …'. The other writer, discoursing on fashions, laments the fact that women were no longer wearing shawls in the old graceful style: 'we now see [them] desecrated; the beautiful Indian Cashmere gathered at the waist and arranged as a *casaque*, not cut, but so disposed as to fit at the back, while falling loose in front, with ample sleeves gathered up at the bend of the arm.' Indeed, she was right and from around this time shawls began to be made into dressing gowns, jackets and even copes and, as a final indignity, to be used as curtains or piano covers.

WOVEN SHAWLS

The early years of the shawl industry were spent addressing the problems of adapting existing looms to weave Indian-style patterns, and finding yarn for spinning that was as soft and fine as that found in the Himalayas. The fleeces from different breeds of sheep were tried, and goats were imported from India with poor results. The earliest manufacturers discovered that a warp of fine silk with a weft

A beautiful turnover shawl with a 'jigsaw' design made by the firm of Richard Shaw of Norwich in the 1830s. This firm was renowned for the very strong-coloured borders on its shawls. (Carrow House Textile Collection. Norfolk Museums 365.981)

of Southdown wool produced the best results. This was a solution arrived at readily in Norwich, where half-silks had been woven for generations. Later, some shawls were woven with a spun silk field and sewn-on silk borders with the design in wool. Others were of wool only or of wool with cotton, while the last and possibly finest of the Norwich shawls in the 1860s and 1870s were woven either of

A silk turnover shawl with a well-designed corner and an architectural type border, probably Norwich, 1830s. (Private collection)

One of nine motifs in this shawl, which was probably cut from a length of fabric, or yardage. Norwich, c.1830. (Private collection)

silk alone or, in the slightly cheaper variety, of silk with some wool. During the hundred years or so of manufacture nearly every possible combination of silk, cotton and wool was tried, depending on the yarn most easily obtained in the district, and for which end of the market the shawls were intended.

The manufacture of shawls was fitted into an industry that had existed for many years and so in each of the main centres early attempts at copying Indian examples were made on the type of loom that could already be found in the locality – damask looms in Edinburgh, draw looms in Norwich, and lappet and harness looms in Paisley. By the early years of the nineteenth century draw or harness looms were being used in all three centres, and in Paisley shawls woven on these looms were often called *harness shawls*. In a harness loom, *harness* refers to the extra mechanism needed to control the lifting of the warps to produce the patterns, but the loom is exactly the same as a draw loom.

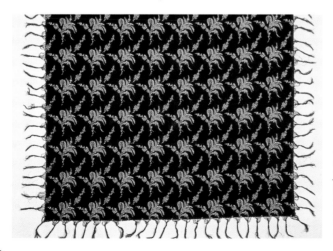

A shawl cut from yardage. The effect of flying is helped by the fillover using both single and double thread. Probably made by Willett & Nephew, Norwich, 1843. (Carrow House Textile Collection. Norfolk Museums 641.965)

22

A square shawl, 1840s, possibly by Willett & Nephew of Norwich. The Norwich red ground is covered with sprigs, larger round the edges and in the corners. (Private collection)

It was not until the late 1820s and the 1830s that the Jacquard loom (invented in France in 1802) was accepted in the shawl industry in Britain. This was a system which did away with the need for a drawboy, whose job was to pull the cords of the harness, by the use of many cards strung together to control the design. Each card was punched with a series of holes which formed one row of the pattern and the needles of the shaft either dropped or did not drop. Where they could go through the holes, the warp was raised, allowing the shuttle to travel across, and thus forming a pattern. The Jacquard loom sped up the weaving and, although drawboys were no longer used, it created the need for other workers such as card-punchers and card-lashers, who put the cards in sequence. These were skilled jobs as the designs had to be read off correctly by the card-punchers, and the correctness of the finished shawls depended more on their work than on that of the weavers.

A square shawl, 1844, made by Towler, Campin, Shickle & Matthews of Norwich. The striking colour of the ground is Norwich red, a colour perfected by the dyeing firm of Michael Stark, the first to be able to dye a mixture of silk and wool exactly the same colour. (Private collection)

A silk turnover shawl with an unusual but very well-managed corner of two different designs, 1830s. (Private collection)

Below: A plaid produced for the 1867 International Exhibition with the name of the manufacturer, D. Spiers & Company, woven into the inside corner. (Paisley Museum and Art Galleries DS25)

Below: *One of the few shawls that can be safely attributed to Willett & Nephew of Norwich, 1840. (Carrow House Textile Collection. Norfolk Museums 1991.66)*

A beautiful shawl with a mirror-image design on a cream ground made by Towler & Campin in 1845, registered design number 25053; silk warp, wool weft, with wool fillover. (Carrow House Textile Collection. Norfolk Museums 1994.64)

A striking design by Clabburn, Son & Crisp of Norwich, 1865–70, showing the same motifs already seen in their other shawls, but reorganised into a very effective whole. (Private collection)

Weaving had been a cottage industry performed by outworkers but Jacquard looms, with their extra mechanism, were too tall to fit into ordinary weavers' houses, and small factories began to be built to accommodate them. The size of these gradually increased, making the use of power practicable, until by the 1860s the norm was for the weaver to go to work in an adapted or purpose-built factory and watch several machines rather than weave by hand in his own home. Though there were still a number of hand-looms, on the whole by the 1860s hand weaving had given way to factory production.

Shawls also became bigger and designs ever more complex, and manufacturers still looked for a way in which the back could be as attractive as the front in order to do away with the need for a pair of shawls (as was the custom in India) or having to fold the shawl in half (as was usual in Britain). It was not until the 1840s that a manufacturer in Paisley, John Cunningham, was able to develop a shawl woven with a pattern on both sides as distinct from one cropped at the back, and in 1854 W. H. Clabburn of Norwich invented a truly reversible shawl. However, neither of these inventions was a commercial success as they came too late.

PRINTED SHAWLS

The popularity of imported Indian calicoes in the eighteenth century encouraged British manufacturers to print similar patterns for the European market. From the end of the eighteenth century fashionable and workaday shawls were decorated with multicoloured designs on a variety of qualities of fabric. Block-cutters were employed to incise wooden blocks, which reproduced the range of colours required for hand-printing the design directly on to the surface of the cloth.

Some early shawls had narrow printed borders of small designs stitched on to plain centres of fabric. During the first quarter of the nineteenth century, as the skill of the block-maker increased, intricate blocks to which metal strips and pins had been added were able to reproduce designs that required fine lines, hatched areas and graded shadows. These arrangements created deep borders of motifs, with rising galleries (between the border and centre), which encroached into plain centres. They were printed directly on to fabric to make square shawls. By the middle of the nineteenth century large, long shawls were printed with borders, galleries, and complex scrolling designs that covered the entire face of the cloth.

Left: *A printed square shawl with a plain centre and a very heavy outside decoration of angled blocks. Probably from Paisley. (Private collection)*

A rare mourning shawl in black and white. Turnover shawl, Norwich, c.1830. (Private collection)

Left: *A discharge-printed shawl of the 1830s, unusual because the fabric is silk damask. Probably made by E. T. Blakely of Norwich. (Carrow House Textile Collection. Norfolk Museums 39.963.3)*

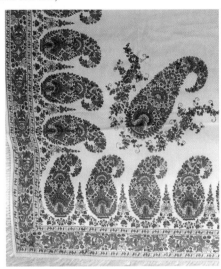

Above: *A square printed shawl, probably from Norwich, c.1840s. There is a small blue line at the bottom of each pine that appears to act as a stand and is possibly the hallmark of the designer. Excellent printing. (Private collection)*

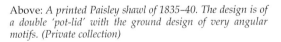

Above: *A printed Paisley shawl of 1835–40. The design is of a double 'pot-lid' with the ground design of very angular motifs. (Private collection)*

A printed long scarf of gauze woven by Towler, Campin & Company of Norwich, 1835–40. In this, as in all their silk scarves and shawls of fine silk, gauze or leno, there is a double thickness of weaving just inside the edges, about 2–3 inches (50–75 mm) wide and usually 1–3 inches (25–75 mm) from the edge. This was to reduce the risk of the frail fabric being torn. (Private collection)

27

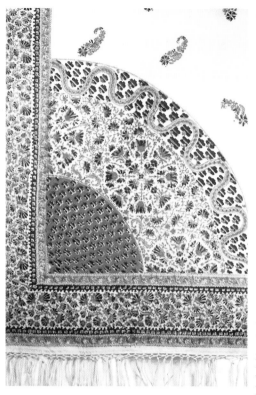

A printed shawl of the 1840s, probably manufactured by E. & F. Hinde of Norwich, for whom the donor's great-grandmother worked. It is of 'pot-lid' design without the usual central circle. (Carrow House Textile Collection. Norfolk Museums 619.972.1)

Dating block-printed shawls is difficult, though size and design style can be useful indications. It was expensive to have sets of blocks made to print perhaps up to eight colours. Changes in fashion could make a design unpopular, prompting manufacturers to store blocks in the hope of running the design at a later date with different colourings. New arrangements of patterns on shawls were also made by printing blocks of contemporary designs and adding others made for earlier styles. This can be seen in shawls where the border and motif differ in design character. By using block-printing, a quicker and cheaper product was possible than by weaving similar patterns on the loom. Towards the middle of the nineteenth century, when high-quality woven shawls had become very fashionable, summer shawls of lightweight material as well as heavier shawls were printed with groups of hatched lines blocked over the designs, to simulate the surface of a twill-woven cloth.

The corner of a beautifully printed shawl, c.1845–50, with the Christmas-tree design. (Carrow House Textile Collection. Norfolk Museums 2000.140)

Above: *Part of one half of a block-printed Arab shawl, c.1859. This must have been for winter wear as instead of being made of gauze it has a silk warp and wool weft. (Carrow House Textile Collection. Norfolk Museums 137.15)*

Below left: *A block-printed shawl with an unusual use of border blocks, possibly 1830–40. (Private collection)*

Below right: *A block-printed shawl, 1850s, strongly resembling those printed by E. T. Blakely of Norwich. (Carrow House Textile Collection. Norfolk Museums 253.981)*

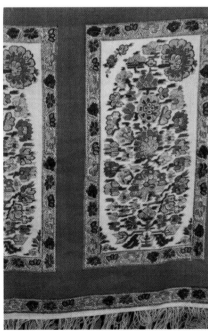

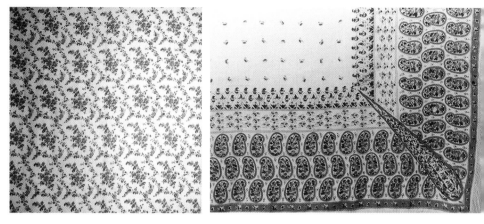

Above left: *A charming shawl cut from yardage and roller-printed, c.1850. (Private collection)*

Above right: *A printed square shawl resembling the Paisley Stanhope design of 1846. (Private collection)*

Below left: *A gauze Arab shawl, c.1860, showing the curved and the square ends, probably from Norwich. (Private collection)*

Below right: *This printed wool design is in a Paisley pattern book with no attribution. The length of the shawl is twice its width and the design is very formal. (Private collection)*

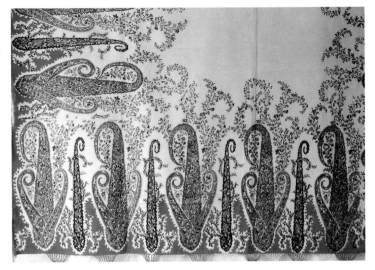

A square printed shawl. The five long pine motifs start from the left of the shawl on each side. (Private collection)

There was a considerable range in the quality of printing done to meet the demands of the market. To satisfy an exclusive clientele, complex patterns had to be well designed and a high standard of precise printing was required. Some shawls have been printed with very sophisticated designs on the finest fabrics and are beautiful examples of the work of master printers. Others have been crudely printed, using clumsy designs on harsh cloth, with carelessly registered colours and badly overlapping corners. The evenness or patchiness of the colour patterns on the reverse side of block-printed cloth can be an indication of the printer's skill.

31

COLOUR, DESIGN AND ATTRIBUTION

The absolute attribution of shawls is always difficult as far too little is known about individual manufacturers and their idiosyncrasies. Dating a shawl approximately is less difficult as there were specific fashions in colour and shape that followed the trends in dress.

Colour

At the beginning of the nineteenth century it was difficult to dye different yarns the same colour and so the majority of long shawls made with a silk warp and wool weft were cream with richly coloured wool patterns (or *fillovers* as they were known in Norwich). Where a strongly coloured shawl was needed it was made with a plain spun-silk field surrounded by a narrow sewn-on patterned border. Often these borders were made by outworkers, which explains why sometimes neither the colours nor the designs quite match. These shawls were usually small and square, with the centres purple, crimson, cinnamon or a favourite shade of strong, slightly bluish pink.

By the 1820s the long shawl was more fashionable than the square. In Scotland the *kirking shawl* became an essential part of the trousseau of a young bride, who wore it to church after her wedding. It was white with a deep end border predominantly dark blue with some crimson and green. The design is often so arranged that the pine shape appears most clearly in the background, white – the *voided pine* design. Whether this was made in Norwich and

A well-loved shawl of the 1830s cut up and mounted as a cape in the second half of the nineteenth century. (Carrow House Textile Collection. Norfolk Museums 2000.122)

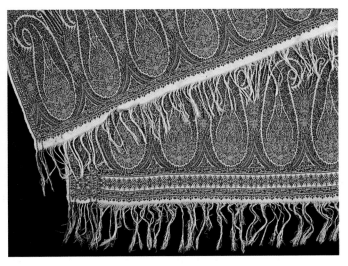

An interesting pair of shawls showing virtually identical designs but slightly different borders. (Paisley Museum and Art Galleries CS19)

Edinburgh as well as Paisley is uncertain.

In the 1830s some shawls had a black ground, and the colour known as *Norwich red* made its appearance. This, in contrast to the more general pinks and crimsons, was a real pillar-box red.

With the use of the Jacquard loom and the greater complexity of design, colours tended to become turgid. There were so many tiny dots of varying colours making up the large designs that where the patterns covered most of the ground the colours merged, giving a rather muddy effect. This, in the 1850s and 1860s, was more noticeable in Paisley shawls. In Norwich shawls, the colours, though tending the same way, managed to keep clearer, especially in silk shawls of the 1860s and 1870s, where crimson, not Norwich red, predominates.

A Jacquard reversible shawl made of double cloth in tabby weave, probably by C. & T. Bolingbroke & Jones, 1860s. (Carrow House Textile Collection. Norfolk Museums 64.983)

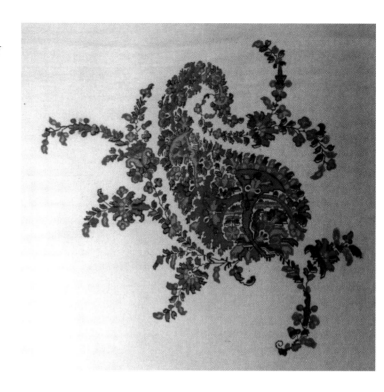

A single motif, printed on yardage, of pure wool; part of a large design. Probably from Norwich, 1840s. (Private collection)

Design

Attribution is often just as difficult where design is concerned. Shawls made in Britain usually imitated those from 'India', and every manufacturer studied the ones that arrived from Kashmir and northern India closely so that patterns tended to resemble one another, wherever the shawls were made. Many designers were freelance, working for several manufacturers. Although what may be called the 'handwriting' of specific designers stands out, we can often only group together a series of shawls as being definitely by the same designer but still cannot identify with any certainty the manufacturer or centre of origin.

In Britain the technical ability of the weavers was considered more important than design. As early as 1760 the Board of Trustees for Agriculture and Fisheries in Edinburgh promoted an academy of design for textiles among other things, but this had a rather chequered existence before it merged in 1858 with the School of Art. However, the Board did appreciate good design and awarded many premiums for it in shawls as in other textiles. In Norwich less attention was paid to design until the founding of the School of Art in 1845, and even then there was much criticism that students spent far too long drawing from ancient casts rather than designing for the applied arts and crafts.

A printed silk leno shawl with a design made from a combination of two designs registered at the Patents Office (registered design numbers 75614 and 75612) by Towler & Campin in 1851. A design, once registered, could be used on different shawls in different ways. (Carrow House Textile Collection. Norfolk Museums 863.967.1)

It was very different in France. From the seventeenth century onwards design had been considered an integral part of manufacture and never more so than in weaving. And it is clear that the British often went to France for their designs. Mr Macdonald of Gibb & Macdonald of Edinburgh travelled to Paris every year after 1815 for designs, while in Paisley a weaver named Holdway was given £40 by the Board of Trustees to study shawls in France. In the 1834 shawl accounts of Grout & Company of Norwich and Yarmouth there is the entry '6 French Hkfs bot for Patterns'.

French designs were also influenced by those on Indian shawls. The magazine *Musée des Dessinateurs de Fabrique* has illustrations of designs in its 1837 numbers with the captions *Motifs levés sur un châle fabriqué en Kashmir* ('Motifs copied from a shawl made in Kashmir') and *...sur des châles de l'Inde* ('... copied from Indian shawls'). Many British shawls, in particular those of Towler & Campin of Norwich, have very similar patterns, suggesting the British manufacturers also knew of these designs and either copied or adapted them.

Although it is difficult to identify the manufacturer from the design, Paisley Museum has several books of original designs dating

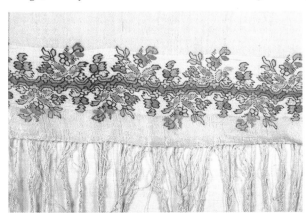

A light summer leno shawl with a narrow border, manufactured and registered by Towler & Campin of Norwich in 1851, registered design number 75613. (Carrow House Textile Collection. Norfolk Museums 751.967.1)

Left: *Half a long shawl, 1869–70, by Towler, Rowling & Allan. The shawl has at some time been cut in half, probably because it was one of the prototypes of the shawl given by Norwich to Queen Victoria on her visit there in 1870. (Carrow House Textile Collection. Norfolk Museums 182.976)*

Above: *A very unusual design for a British shawl, strongly resembling a Mughal (Indian) design of the seventeenth century; woven by Towler, Campin, Shickle & Matthews of Norwich, 1844. Now cut up into a waistcoat. (Private collection)*

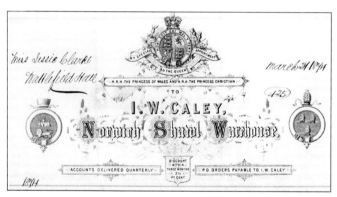

A bill heading of I. W. Caley, Norwich Shawl Warehouse, 1874. (Private collection)

A silk shawl by Clabburn, Son & Crisp, 1860s, showing back and front, and possible to wear both ways. Later adapted for a bedspread. (Carrow House Textile Collection. Norfolk Museums 347.984.15)

from between 1825 and 1850, and a number of these show the name of the designer plus the firm which used them. For example, Forbes Chinery & Company and John Morgan & Company are two firms mentioned. In Edinburgh a number of shawls together with sample borders from Gibb & Macdonald were examined and photographed by the Museum of the Antiquities of Scotland in 1973. Norfolk Museums have an 1830 pattern book of Richard Shaw, a local manufacturer, which shows many of the designs he used.

In 1842 a Parliamentary Commission reported on 'The State of Hand-loom Weaving' and as a result manufacturers were allowed to register their designs at the Patent Office for a term of three or six months. Comparatively few manufacturers availed themselves of this concession, but there are 315 designs registered from Norwich and many more from Paisley dating from between 1843 and 1875. A considerable number of Norwich shawls have already been checked from this source.

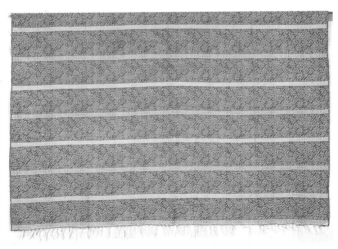

A shawl made at the end of the period by Clabburn, Son & Crisp. It shows that by the 1880s manufacturers were well aware that shawls were going out of fashion, so they hedged their bets. This fabric can be found as shawls with different coloured stripes or quite plain, all cut from yardage, and the plain fabric was also suitable for up-holstery or curtains. (Private collection)

A cope made from a Norwich shawl, c.1870. The cope was made c.1950. (Private collection)

Below: The label on a shawl made by Clabburn, Son & Crisp and sold by the retailer Caley Bros. (Carrow House Textile Collection. Norfolk Museums 614.978.2)

Below: Shawl, 1845–50, made by E. & F. Hinde of Norwich, known as 'Arab' in Norwich, 'Glasgow' in Paisley, and 'burnous' in textile literature. Shawls such as this were made in two halves, with a different design in each, and so could be worn in different ways. (Private collection)

A rare Norwich shawl by E. T. Blakely of black cashmere wool with silk patterning. It has the unusual addition of gold thread in the inner border and outlining the pine motifs. This innovative shawl was shown at the Great Exhibition of 1851 and was commented on favourably, but it seems that only a few were made for sale. (Private collection)

It is sometimes suggested that all shawls with a pine-cone motif are 'Paisley shawls'. For anyone who knows the history of the industry, this is far from true. A shawl made in Norwich is a Norwich shawl, one made in Edinburgh an Edinburgh shawl. And, after all, they were all, whether from Norwich, Edinburgh or Paisley, made originally 'in imitation of the Indian'.

PLACES TO VISIT

Most costume museums have several shawls but they are not usually displayed as a collection in their own right and may not even be on show. Some shawls will be found at the museums listed here; those marked with an asterisk* hold the most comprehensive collections of shawls. It is essential that serious students telephone to arrange a visit. Other visitors are advised to telephone before they travel, in order to find out the dates and times of opening.

Bankfield Museum, Boothtown Road, Halifax, West Yorkshire HX3 6HG. Telephone: 01422 354823.

Gallery of Costume, Platt Hall, Rusholme, Manchester M14 5LL. Telephone: 0161 224 5217. Website: www.cityartgalleries.org.uk

Museum of Costume, The Assembly Rooms, Bennett Street, Bath, Somerset BA1 2QH. Telephone: 01225 477789. Website: www.museumofcostume.co.uk

*Paisley Museum and Art Galleries**, High Street, Paisley, Renfrewshire PA1 2BA. Telephone: 0141 889 3151. Website: www.renfrewshire.gov.uk

Potteries Museum and Art Gallery, Bethesda Street, Hanley, Stoke-on-Trent, Staffordshire ST1 3DE. Telephone: 01782 232323. Website: www.stoke.gov.uk/museums

*Textile and Costume Study Centre**, Carrow House, King Street, Norwich, Norfolk NR1 2TN. Telephone: 01603 223870 (booking required). (The costume department of Norfolk Museums and Archaeology Service.)

*Victoria and Albert Museum**, Cromwell Road, South Kensington, London SW7 2RL. Telephone: 020 7942 2000. Website: www.vam.ac.uk

York Castle Museum, Eye of York, York YO1 9RY. Telephone: 01904 653611. Website: www.york.gov.uk

A silk scarf made from shawl fabric, c.1890, possibly for the Indian market. It has been suggested that these long narrow scarfs, when exported, were worn by men as double waistbands. (Private collection)